RIPE

The Felix Pollak Prize in Poetry

THE UNIVERSITY OF WISCONSIN PRESS POETRY SERIES

RONALD WALLACE, GENERAL EDITOR

Now We're Getting Somewhere * David Clewell
Henry Taylor, Judge, 1994

The Legend of Light * Bob Hicok
Carolyn Kizer, Judge, 1995

Fragments in Us: Recent and Earlier Poems * Dennis Trudell
Philip Levine, Judge, 1996

Don't Explain * Betsy Sholl
Rita Dove, Judge, 1997

Mrs. Dumpty * Chana Bloch
Donald Hall, Judge, 1998

Liver * Charles Harper Webb
Robert Bly, Judge, 1999

Ejo * Derick Burleson
Alicia Ostriker, Judge, 2000

Borrowed Dress * Cathy Colman
Mark Doty, Judge, 2001

Ripe * Roy Jacobstein
Edward Hirsch, Judge, 2002

RIPE

Roy Jacobstein

The University of Wisconsin Press

The University of Wisconsin Press
1930 Monroe Street
Madison, Wisconsin 53711

www.wisc.edu/wisconsinpress/

3 Henrietta Street
London WC2E 8LU, England

Printed in the United States of America

Library of Congress Cataloging-in-Publication Data
Jacobstein, Roy.
Ripe / Roy Jacobstein.
p. cm. — (The Felix Pollak prize in poetry)
ISBN 0–299–18250–9 (cloth: alk. paper) —
ISBN 0–299–18254–1 (pbk.: alk. paper)
I. Title. II. Felix Pollak prize in poetry (Series)
PS3610.A3568 R57 2002
811'.6dc21
2002004976

for David and Sophie-Anne,

and for Linda Ippolito, ora e per sempre

෨

. . . delight,

Since the imperfect is so hot in us,

Lies in flawed words and stubborn sounds.

—WALLACE STEVENS, "The Poems of Our Climate"

Contents

THREE

Acknowledgments

Thanks to the following teachers who read some or all of these poems and offered suggestions for improvement: Agha Shahid Ali, David Baker, Roger Fanning, Linda Gregerson, Mary Leader, Thomas Lux, Steve Orlen, Martha Rhodes, Eleanor Wilner, and Dean Young. Thanks too to Ellen Bryant Voigt and the rest of the Warren Wilson College M.F.A. Program's community of writers for immeasurably enhancing my writing path.

Grateful acknowledgement is also made to the editors of the following publications where these poems, some of which have been revised, first appeared:

The Beloit Poetry Journal: "What It Was"
The Gettysburg Review: "Autumn Geometric," "Beyond the Gauze Curtain,"
    "Parting Conversation"
Graven Images: "The Lesson"
Green Mountains Review: "The Cardplayers"
Gulf Coast: "Home Run"
JAMA: "Dutch Landscape"
Luna: "La Création"
The Marlboro Review: "Reincarnation"
Mediphors: "Admissions"
Mid-American Review: "Swale"
Nimrod: "Passover," "There Is No Point in Time"
Parnassus: "Why Not Write a Novel"
Poetry Northwest: "Free Hermit Crab"
Prairie Schooner: "Chartreuse," "Marvelous the Myriad Forms," "Ripe,"
    "See You," "Sto Lat"
Puerto del Sol: "Calamari"
Quarterly West: "Nuclear Family Vacation Blues," "Rooting"
River City: "This Way to the Egress"

Sarasota Review of Poetry: "Election Day, Washington D.C.," "Morning Flight"

Solo: "Coming of Age"

The Southeast Review: "Across from Holy Name Hospital"

The Threepenny Review: "Bypass," "The Odd Morphology of Regret"

Witness: "Atomic Numbers," "Near Rusomo," "Pre-Med," "Safari, Rift Valley,"
"'Squid's Sex Life Revealed' in USA TODAY"

Wordwrights: "Magnetic Field," "The Mugging," "My Woman Is Like
Nevada," "Time-Lapse"

"Swale" was awarded the *James Wright Poetry Prize.*

"Reincarnation" was runner-up for the *Marlboro Prize in Poetry.*

"Autumn Geometric" was featured on *Poetry Daily.*

ONE

Chartreuse

The finches must be migrating North again.
There! someone points, and at last I see it

in the quivering backdrop of backlit leaves—
and immediately I think of my mother

because it's the color she called *chartreuse*,
looking up at me from her magnifying glass

and sheaf of French exams to affix that word
to the '58 Chevy my father brought home.

Everything was a forest then, impenetrable
as the upper Amazon, our modern parents

raising us beneath the icy aegis of science:
it wasn't *pee-pee* and *poop*, it was *urinate*

and *defecate, penis* and *vagina*, yet never
a hint of the mechanics or mess of sex, so

what else could I do but attend med school
to learn *left supra-clavicular notch*

was the name for that soft indentation above
the collarbone whence I'd thought for years

babies must come, knowing even then
they must come from somewhere deep

within the woman's body. Yes, it was all
so abstruse, but now my dictionary yields

memory's precise hue—it's *a clear light green*
with a yellowish tinge, color of the aromatic

liqueur made by the Carthusian monks
at Grenoble, France, and you ease its top

shoulder down and bottom shoulder up
to guide it safely from the birth canal, out

into this numinous world of sun and finch,
Amazon and oak, of stillness and motion,

nest and migration, of source and shadow,
instrument and accident, of holding on

and letting go.

Atomic Numbers

Mr. Gardner in 10th grade told us there was no purpose
to mitochondria, just function. Your lungs turn black
in a day if you smoke, black as that ink streaking
your sorry hands, thundered bald Mr. Strepek in Print Shop,
and stay black five years, even if a cigarette never touches
your lips again, and your breath stinks too. But Karen took
Home Ec., so she kept flicking Virginia Slims from the pack,
blowing onion rings into my face. Miss Testasecca taught us
the tangent is a function of the right triangle. Miss Piilo
made us memorize atomic numbers. Uranium: Number 235—
no wonder it's radioactive. Pb, sign for lead, stood for something
like *plumbus* in Latin—or was it Greek? After semester break
she came back as Mrs. Giglio. *Lily,* she told us it meant
in Italian, turning to write a formula on the blackboard,
tugging at her tightened skirt. Things are getting tougher
all the time, Chucky Klein quipped. Years later he got
himself shot reporting Jonestown, survived, moved to TV.
I want to ask old Mr. Curran right now, How come *The Lord
of the Flies* has to have Piggy drop those glasses and why
did that 17-year-old leave her newborn girl in the dumpster
last week and what'll they do to her now? Who's the *rough
beast* he'd say in that brogue that caressed us like the tongue
of a cat. Some days you just want to be toes, curled inward
or pressed against another warm body until first recess crawls
by—then Mr. Adamson's supposed to teach us how to shift
from second to third and accelerate into the straightaway.

Pre-Med

All semester in Psych Lab I shocked
the nictitating membrane of a white rabbit
(every ten seconds for seven minutes).
Our professor was making his name
puréeing smart planaria and feeding them
to dumb ones who then became smart.
It all had to do with DNA and learning
and memory, as I recall, and maybe
the Pill, or possibly the pacification plan
for Vietnam. Deliver direct electrical current—
It's mild, he assured us—to that opaque bit
of ocular tissue, then enter the subjects'
responses into the charts in our cross-hatched
notebooks. I recall the experimenter (E—me)
seemed upset, far more distressed
than the subject (S: sleek fur, berry eyes),
though in time E would master the art of labeling
someone else's pain *a little discomfort.*

Coming of Age

We head to Fred's Beds
for a futon, our first joint
purchase. She's left the attic
of Joan's Reducing Studio
to live with me in my room
atop Jewell's Hand Massage.
I've always been nuts,
she said, for a guy who plays
harmonica. With luck, in moth-
light, we'll make love on it
for the length of the three-year
warranty before we graduate
to mattress, box springs,
sleeping with somebody else.

Admissions

To do . . . to doo . . . what to doo,
to doo . . . I don't know what
to doo, to doo . . . to dooo, moans

Hector nonstop, his moans curling
counterclockwise along the corridor,
dragging us with him through his day-

long night, as we interns round on
the latest admissions: the cheerleader
O.D.'ed on spurned love and Tylenol,

the seizure disorder from Hornell—
a visitation from God, his mother
says, the one who knows me

and wants to paint me as Jesus
(long hair, black beard, and all).
In the treatment room they're piercing

the spine of the next new leukemic:
her back curves across the exam table
like a slice of cantaloupe on a plate.

Above us, TVs flicker—another game
show. Nurses wheel drug carts, I.V. poles;
shift succeeds shift. Over everything,

that ceaseless droning—Hector Arroyo,
age 9, demented, gone to encephalitis.
And at the rear of the little troupe,

fingering his stethoscope's dark rubber
the way a snake-charmer fingers his flute,
a 25-year-old boy sweating his lines, sweat

lining the back of his short white coat, a secret
charter member of *The Hector Arroyo Club*
who wonders what they'll stick into him

when no cobra dances from the straw basket.

Dutch Landscape

You lie upstairs in a king-sized bed
while fluid the color of weak tea
seeps into your pleural cavities
and stains your breath.
In the living room below, your son,
Simon—*sea-moan* in Dutch—
pedals his red trike in circles
on the bare wood floor
and Piaf hunkers at my feet—

Piaf, who frisked down center aisle
of the Pieterskerk and leapt
when we threw the rice.
Beyond the long window
a lone duck drifts
the murky water of the Prinsengracht
and the cobblestones glisten,
as they do here in Amsterdam
after the rain.

Once, working the swing shift
at Dodge Main, I'd fit the gray lips
of the spot welder over twin steel plates
twenty-three times an hour.
Trip the trigger and arcs of flame
fuse the plates in a shiver of sparks.
But Dodge Main's been razed for years,
my welding guns gone for scrap.
I can join life to no one.

What It Was

Often, at Strong Memorial Hospital,
I'd guide a 15-gauge needle into the center
of a child's lower back. It was so easy,
any time I wanted I could slip it in,
between the vertebral ridges of L2 and L3,
blindfolded even, feel the pop, and presto—
cerebrospinal fluid dripping out. I never could
get the nurses to believe the kid
did not have acute leukemia. They knew
the drill: slap on the purple label,
call the *stat* messenger, console the parents
waiting for the test results, a flotilla
of 100,000 deranged cells per cubic centimeter
pouring from Mona's marrow or Phil's spleen
into the bloodstream. After my latest 36-hour day,
sun risen, set, risen, set, I'd arrive home,
smelling of night rattles and slow clocks
and sodden scrambled eggs, and slip
into my then-wife's arms, wanting only
to be told what it wasn't. But all she said
before I went under, swimming her reefs
without aqualung or mask, was what it was.

Magnetic Field

Sixteen years, Doug, you dumb fuck.
Sixteen years ago—not on a day
like today: gray, planed by wind,
squeezed in the vise of February,
violet worms clotting the sidewalk,
the dank air, with their earth-slime
stink, a day anyone could fathom
sighting down the wrong end
of twin barrels.
          No, one of those
days of blossom, an irruption
of rhododendron and redbud,
one of those days lovers crave.
You should know the eyelids
Dad passed on to both of us
sag, Doug, just like his did,
and the crows that still blacken
our sycamores caw *ought, ought.*

Across from Holy Name Hospital

What's semiotics to a cat?
Splayed on your lap, her four limbs
to the four winds, no language

conditions her thought, no doubt
the bobbing branch bobs. She takes it
all in, all of it her due, until *better*

tempts those tawny semaphores
ever attuned to what is, and she's off,
leaving us to our signs:

Quiet, Zone, needle, mass.
True, there's still the world rolling
from your nib, the world you make

as you like, a world of whatever
you choose to fix: cinnamon toast,
or purple crocus, bent on return.

You can make anything you want,
you can call anything out, have it
scutter past in the mist—

sand crab, storm cloud, cat, Mother
Superior (wimple and jowl)—
anything at all, but the gone

remain gone, all the holy names.

—*Ethel Ippolito, 1933–1998*

Why Not Write a Novel

Make it historical. Akhmatova doesn't return
to Petersburg and Modigliani doesn't succumb

to TB. They take a ramshackle villa near Lucca.
She pens odes to the future, to oregano, *noirs*

under a pseudonym. He paints her angular
Slavic cheeks, that long lean body, draped

in electric blue. Picasso and Diaghilev make
cameos. Amedeo fleshes out his nudes,

accommodating Anna and her swelling belly.
Marina and Nikolai follow fast on the heels

of little Sergei, and all goes well for a while
but then—what? Envying gods? *Il diavolo?*

The basic fuck-up of forty-six chromosomes?
Something—that stealthy certain something—

slips in. Amedeo trysts with the lithe *ragazza*
and her auburn hair. Anna banks fire with fire,

and free love isn't, not now, when the *bambini*
need looking after and Amedeo's not selling

and no one, even in this fiction, reads poems—
and anyway the storm clouds are goose-stepping

through Umbria, because you can only change
so much, and if the TB didn't get Amedeo,

his circumcised dick would, and Anna
would be lined up in the predawn frost

before a different pack of thugs, waiting
to ask about her missing men again.

Near Rusomo

A.P. Wire Photo, The New York Times, 12/21/97

> *People say they have to express their emotions.*
> *I'm sick of that. Photography doesn't teach you*
> *to express your emotions; it teaches you how to see.*
> —BERENICE ABBOTT

They're downstream now,
beyond the falls,
eight or ten, or more,
out of the turbulence.
The Kagera River churns
onward into Tanzania, leaving
them behind in the backwash.
The smooth stone outcropping
of their native land hovers
over them like a mother seal.
They huddle against her
black flanks the way they leaned
into one another last week
in the Church for safety
in numbers. And now
that the machetes have passed,
the torsos are looking down
into the debris-choked shallows
for their missing heads and limbs.

Sto Lat

"Long life," the Polish toast to good health,
literally, "one hundred years."

—To the memory of Robert Desnos

Your "Voice" comes late, Robert, here
in a converted barn at a writers' conference,
amid the litany of concentration camps
rattling the loose windows, the names
of many unknown to me, a child
of the mild and mundane Midwest, born
after the ovens had cooled, their vapors
curling no longer out of Europe's voiceless mouth,
over the Black Madonna's saltless tears.

There were blue numbers on the ventral surface
of her right arm, my mother-in-law-to-be,
that spring day in 1970. Her daughter, Shoshana,
the one the few survivors from Radom
said was *Manya's exact double,*
stood beneath the canopy, Detroit Shaarey Zedek,
and heard the rabbi say "Repeat after me, in Hebrew
and then English, *Anee l'dodee v'dodee lee*—
I am my beloved's as my beloved is mine."
I too was learning new words:
lesion, necrosis, dysmorphic, ventral.

I pay tribute to you Manya, Manushka, Maria,
grandmother of my son,
I thank God you spoke flawlessly
that guttural tongue I can never hear
without hearing *round them up,*
spoke so fluently you and your blue eyes passed,

and even when they could pass no longer,
still, at Auschwitz, they were passport
to the office job, the occasional German kindness
of warm roll, a hard-boiled egg,
just as there must have been at Auschwitz
a sunny day, sunny days,
the kind of day where anywhere on Earth
long life seems possible.

I pay tribute to you, Robert,
reading the fortunes of your fellow travelers—headed
where?—Birkenau, Belsen, Treblinka, Terezin?
Even in the boxcars you trailed your index finger
along the smooth palms of the young,
the creases and fissures of the old,
predicting in a low voice, over the clacketing rails,
in French, your mother tongue, the language
of Piaf and Pétain, to one and all, *long life.*

To all those smiling Cambodians
to whom I spoke in stilting Khmer
in the refugee camps at Khao-I-Dang and Nong Khai,
and those in the transit camp at Pinatnikom, the ones
whose smile Pol Pot could not efface,
behind whose teeth every tongue,
every bitten tongue, held its tale of loss
(buried in the graceful splay of the dancers' fingers,
the artificial fingernails, curved backward, painted gold,
the dances for birth, for rebirth, for harvest): tribute.

To that one specific woman, her name long flown,
who came to the makeshift delivery room, abdomen swollen
well beyond the nine-month gravid girth
the obstetrics text told us to expect,
and delivered, without anesthesia, without a sound,
a boy without a brain, and got up off the table

and smiled at me, made the *wai* of respect,
eyes cast down, palms pressed above her bowed head,
and, still saying nothing, returned
to the straw pallet in the thatched-roof tent
where her husband and mother and child awaited her,
where she'd slept each night the past two years: tribute.

It is true—the hacked and mutilated in Kigali,
the *ethnically cleansed* in all the Srebenicas,
those who survived the Gulag and those who didn't,
the *desaparacidos* of Santiago and Buenos Aires
and the bloody broken wishbone of Central America,
those who fell at Wounded Knee and those who yet stand,
the children of the children of the children
of the slaves who passed through Gorée Island
to become New World dust,
the Armenians Palestinians Tibetans Kashmiris Kurds—
all the tongues, all the words: poetry stops nothing.

I don't know when you were born, Robert.
You wrote the poem we heard today in 1928,
the one where you call out at midnight,
call all to you: *those lost in the fields . . .*
old skeletons . . . young oaks cut down . . .
scraps of cloth rotting on the ground . . .
hangmen pilots bricklayers architects
assassins
the one you love,
three times you call the one you love.

I'd guess you were close to thirty
when you wrote it, maybe twenty-nine,
born in 1899, one hundred years ago.
If they found you in some café, arguing
about Wittgenstein or Nietzsche with your friends,
if you didn't look like a Jew

and none of your neighbors bore you a grudge
or coveted your flat or your goose-neck lamp,
maybe they didn't find you for a while,
until 1942 or '43. That would make you
my age when you boarded the train.

In the grainy flickering silent movie of your life
it would be winter, a gray day, raked by wind,
your black fedora slung low over your brow—
but it wasn't, I can see it, one of those perfect
Parisian days, late spring, 11 A.M.,
the smell of *brioche* on the cobblestones,
the sun bending to kiss the dry earth
like a pilgrim first arrived at Mecca.

Now we enter the next century.
All the future names God alone knows—their names,
the towns, the rivers which will run black—God
and you, Robert, and the darkmost chamber
of every human heart, but you knew all that
even as you went up that rough planking
into the boxcar, and stood with the others
massed there, held on to the side boards
with one hand, the other you took
from your lower back, where the blunt end
of the *Polizei*'s rifle had smashed
into your kidney, your urine will run red,
all this you knew
when you ran your finger along the wrinkled right palm
of the woman with the gold tooth,
looked deep into her deep brown eyes
and predicted *long life,*
and to her twelve-year-old grandson clinging to her side,
long life.

The wheel is turning, Robert.
The next century is upon us.
The knives are glinting and sharp.
The one you loved did not listen.
The one you loved did not hear.
The one you loved did not answer.
I extend my hand to you.

TWO

The Cardplayers

Of course the dead hover close—take my
first cousin, Nelson: he's to be buried later

today in a city five hundred miles from here.
The rabbi will chant the age-old prayers,

those who remain will provide solace.
I know: my mother and father and brother—

cardplayers too—shuffled from the Earth
to the same ceremony. They're here now

in the kitchen. It's my father's deal.
Already Nelson is pulling up his chair,

cutting the deck. Listen to the metal legs
scraping the linoleum, the flutter of the cards

as they fall onto the beige folding table,
the clink of the ice in their glasses,

their laughter filling the living room,
the still air, the red irretrievable dawn.

Rooting

Ardent Cingané, *gypsy* in Turkish,
my three-legged calico cat, presses
her pink nose into my warm armpit.

This must be the single-minded way
pigs in Perigord bulldoze autumn
earth awake in search of truffles,

black as tar, more valuable than gold.
It must be the way the eyes
of that five-year old boy who once

was me raked the munificent grass
for the buried treasure of bottle caps,
his useless clod of an infant brother

nursing away atop an Army blanket.
In Rome, the cells where gladiators
awaited release into the sun-stippled

Colosseum remain darkened, silted-in.
In the Living section of yesterday's *Times*
archaeologists in Jerusalem sift bits

of pre-Canaanite pottery. And somewhere,
in some damp persistent cellar, a poet
roots the humus of memory for the precise

image that will trigger the flow of milk.

Passover

Humming, Aunt Bea ladles *knadlach:*
matzo-ball boulders in a yellow sea.
Soon all four Aunts will rise and merge

again in the kitchen—that long unbroken
lineage: shtetl, sister and steam. Pinochle
will claim the uncles, cousins will scatter,

some to swap baseball cards, some to dress
dolls, but I'll return to the photos,
fixed between those little black triangles.

Here's Uncle Herman's bayonet, gleaming
in the Prussian sun. This one is Uncle Saul,
in the shadows of steerage, his goodbyes

to Smyrna already uttered in four tongues.
And over here, on that railroad platform,
the slim teenager singing for the last Tsar—

Nicholas II, who sits so straight between
his uniformed guards on the royal train—
that's Aunt Bea, at the front of the chorus

of village girls spilling out their dark eyes.

Time-Lapse

Bomber jacket, billowy white scarf,
leather headgear lining his unlined
forehead, light haloing his pinpoint
pupils—in the photo I had framed
he's ready to face the Lüftwaffe solo.
Imagine the sorties over Germany: the Flying

Fortresses opening their bays onto Essen
while he and his P-51 Mustang duel
the Messerschmidts over the Ruhr,
four of those babies flaming down, down—
four more to be rounded up for scrap;
three kills in the raids on Regensburg;
Berlin, again and again, flares
in the night sky, the ack-ack, the tracers.

How many takes did it take at
    The Bach Studio
      SIKESTON
        MO
      June 1943.
How many days until final

flight training, that long slow slide
from the dusty runway, straight
to the base library to check out books
to officers for the duration of the War?
In the darkroom what maneuvers
were needed, father, to airbrush fear?
Were they the same dodgings
and burnings I've made today?

This Way to the Egress

He startles from sleep to scuttering
within the screened-in porch: a bird,

small and brown, its claws frantic,
scraping the meshwork, raising rust.

He turns five today, Columbus Day,
not a major holiday for Detroit, urban

arteries pulsing with brawny Ukranian
tool-and-die-men, Polish spot welders,

the white and black sons of Alabama
and Tennessee, all heeding the siren

call of the Fords. Down the hall he speeds,
past those cheap Picasso prints (jugglers,

harlequins, big-nosed women, fractured
guitars) toward that center that holds

his known world. He bursts in; brakes—
there they are: his father, on top . . .

mother, below . . . grimacing, twisting,
wings flapping beneath the white sheet.

The Lesson

What transgression, Bobby Bordley,
what transgression made fat Mr. Hantler
drop his trowel, his gloves, everything
he was doing that hot May day
to chase you from one end
of Fullerton to the other, trying to
wring your little neck?

The rest of the *Valiants*
stood stupefied on the sidewalk—
livestock stunned before slaughter,
running only in our minds,
but running with you still,
weaving a desperate curlicue
to evade that grown man.

Nothing from that day remains,
not George V Drugs, not the Avalon Theater,
not Mr. Hantler, younger then, no doubt,
than any *Valiant* now.
Not the roses he trimmed so carefully
and watered with his green snake
of garden hose, nor the ball and curse

you hurled into his flower bed.
And Helen Hantler herself must be gray
and stout and almost beyond remembering
how her legs twitched behind the screen door
to see someone—anyone—
escape her father's meaty hands.

There Is No Point in Time

A name surfaces like carp in an ornamental pond, rising
from the deep to the grated fish feed of an eight-beat line.
Never be afraid, Proust says, *to go too far, for truth*

lies beyond, hence this call to him, my oldest friend.
Who else would remember Ting, returning the striped
rubber ball, paw over yellow paw? How does it happen,

one moment on a broiling corner, embroiled in another
spat, the next, two decades gone? Does he remember
when we saw *Morocco,* how Dietrich is left to wander

the desert, trailing Gary Cooper's kepi into the gray
celluloid dusk? Does he remember my tiny mother
taught him *Partir, c'est mourir un peu?* I remember

the *lieder* in his living room. His tenor was so pure . . .
that voice!—can that *cri du chat* be his? Hang up.
Voices, too, must change. No message to leave, no

big deal, *rien,* what can be said in 20 seconds can be
held inside twenty years, though who can say when
a thought of him will come again, bleeding up to feed.

Nuclear Family Vacation Blues

Mariposa, she tells her two fidgeting sons,
means butterfly in *español. Mari* means
husband *en français.* Dad's sacked out

back in Room 3. Long drive in the desert,
Anasazi ruins at Mesa Verde, atomic debris—
they'll do it every time. Mom teaches Romance

Languages, Spanish and French, throws in
some Dante now and then. *Dante al dente*
she calls it. *Esposa* means wife, yet *esposas*

are handcuffs, see? But the boys want pinball
not lessons in sexism. They bound like impala
from the car each night, eager to investigate

their next motel. They love the shuffleboard,
the swimming pools shaped like lima beans,
the chicken-fried steaks in one-light towns—

though Vegas was OK, watching the fruits spin
on the slots, the purple neon splitting the sky.
And sometimes the road kill can be really cool.

The Mugging

He slips through the crack
of the open chained door
and stands above me again,

returned from another day
at *King Lear Men's Wear,*
a day paid out on sales

of shiny lime-green suits
with giant pointed collars,
another day of returns

from stale back rooms, boxed
Arrows stacked high against
his chest. Again I look up, up

to the violet, already-swollen
lids. Again my mother gasps
Your face! His voice is still

a bare black branch snapping
to the weight of ice, snapping
It's nothing . . . leave it alone!

I just banged into a door.

Election Day, Washington, D.C.

It all returns to him in the cafeteria as he waits
to vote. That tiny woman in the hairnet, bent

over her steaming vat—she must have been
Scottish: *Ooh, laddy, want a hut plate?*

The macaroni and cheese, the long wooden
tables gouged with hearts and arrows *(Danny*

& Doreen, 3/17/63, Butchy Loves Beverly
Forever) Post Jr. High: 22 minutes allotted

to erase the Chicken à la King, the Wonder
Bread (a soft slice squeegees the last streaks

of gravy: thick, opaque, the exact faded yellow
of Mr. Franzke's '58 Pontiac) and always

time's left before the next bell to toss the ball
with Storfer and Rickert and Arnold Armstrong

(everyone's best friend in that waning season
of *Negroes*). In his hand, party platforms jostle:

Socialist Workers, New Statehood, UMOJA,
the *Democrats.* He's even taken advice from

the rat he passed (so small and wet, shivering
in the morning rain): *Yes On Subsidized Heat.*

He wonders if rats crouched against the school
wall when his parents went to vote, then shuts

the curtain, eases the ballot into its slot, and punches
out his choice for President with the metal tooth.

Beyond the Gauze Curtain

Everyone seems to have one,
in a position of prominence,
as I do over the wooden mantel
of the gas-fueled fireplace,
a grainy black-and-white photograph
in a gilt-edged frame. A grandparent,
or a more distant ancestor—say, great-
great-grandmother Hannah
from the old country, somewhere
beyond the pale, in what today
might be Belarus. Or maybe it's Maudie
from County Clare, the one who later
headed out to Utah with her Swede.
Or most distant of all, oneself, held aloft
by beaming parents and clutching Bear
with such small hands. Beyond the gauze
curtain, beyond the window, how tall
was the wheat? Where were the wars?
Was it the year cousin Nora eloped
or the year her father died? Everyone
is here before the shutter, as close
as the minute that has just now passed.

Bypass

One day it's Miss Scarlet with
the Candlestick in the Conservatory,
the next they're carting someone
down the corridor to where Dr. Black
with the chisel in the O.R.
waits to crack the vault of a chest.
It's not a calico cat, purring
all night by a child's side,
not acne, not the daily rush
to the job, it's a gurney pulsing
along a narrow passageway,
and it seems you are that someone
for whom the Heart Team scrubs,
a corpuscle the color of dusk,
wanting for air, and no clue
how you got there, nor who waits
so silently behind the next door,
Colonel Mustard or Professor Plum,
come to the Ballroom with the Rope.

Safari, Rift Valley

Minutes ago those quick cleft hoofs
lifted the dik-dik's speckled frame.
Now the cheetah dips her delicate head
to the still-pulsating guts. Our Rover's
so close we need no zoom to fix the green
shot of her eyes, the matted red mess
of her face. You come here, recall a father
hale in his ordinary life, not his last bed,
not the long tasteless slide of tapioca.
This is the Great Rift, where it all began,
here where the warthogs and hartebeest
feed in the scrub, giraffes splay to drink,
and our rank diesel exhaust darkens the air
for only a few moments before vanishing.

THREE

Ripe

Somewhere my father must be
eating the *mooshy* parts of a peach
as a favor for a child,
the way he once did for me.
May it be sunny there, and a lei
of light illumine his brow.
The years it's taken to learn sweetness
resides in the bruises.

Reincarnation

If they're right, this mosquito dive-bombing my ear
into total *presence* at 3 A.M. is Rasputin, or your late

Schnauzer or possibly (why not?) one of those spears
of asparagus served at Cousin Dee's 83rd birthday

luncheon last month, or even Cousin Dee herself,
depending on karmic law and the minute particulars

of the soul's transmigration (interval of dormancy,
if any, distance traversed in space and time, degree

of ascent or descent on the biologic scale from mite
to man, etc.), which means that among this newly

hatched crop of anophelines, who unimpeded live
but a few days, and whose females alone bite, could be

Shakespeare (spiraled down through the centuries) or
the louse that once bit the arse of the unknown (to us)

object of his affection in "Sonnet 55," so on the chance
those who believe this sort of thing—a priori no less

nor more plausible than Red Seas parting or virgin
births or sun gods demanding sacrifice of human

(preferably young and female) flesh—are right,
I'll forbear from further attempts to squash what

well may be Mohandas K. Gandhi, secure in knowing
should I come back as a cat I'll sleep soundly, curled

upon myself on the soft couch while someone's
cousin or mother or child circles overhead

in her newfound brown body, shaking the last
of her human tears from her glistening wings . . .

Swale

Would it have helped if I'd known *swale* meant a low-
lying or depressed and often wet stretch of land? Maybe
I'd have understood her moistures and stoops, though
the word is of Scandinavian origin and I am not. Ah, origins.
I swear we make a mountain of a few inches, a few cells.
If not a mountain, a hillock, a rude mound. Clit or cock,
ermine, stoat, aren't we all just topiary anyway, on the road
to the inner harbor? And speaking of pruning, why did it take
so many years to understand that sign? Every fifth Thursday,
3:30 P.M., there it was, across from DOM & ERNIE'S,
visible as a galaxy of dust motes in a sun-shaft: *We Repair
Non-Union Haircuts.* Like a rune or sentence in need
of a good parsing, I sat on the cracked red leather
of the middle barber's chair, peering out at it, waiting
to be spun around, *voilà*, again a Mexican Hairless,
Dom and my mother doing their polka of delight,
my brain backstroking in the bay of abstraction. True,
its syntax is none too mystic, maybe it was the diction,
how the hell should I know, I was only eight. Befuddlement
ran deep in urban Detroit. Don't you love how *b* and *d* thud by?
And who could forget Henry Ford's goons, there at the factory
overpass, the blood vessels bursting like boils from the worker's
heads at the sight of the truncheons? Well, Dom and Mom could,
evidently, probably Ernie too, hard to say, being he was off
Thursdays. Funny, later I was a Teamster, at the time of the riots.
Local 199—had my union card, but how do we really know
we've made the team? And what's the game, duckpins?
And now that we're approaching the main theme here,
what about the problem of pomegranates—they're so different,
and they come from so far away. Aren't they just like *relationships,*
extraction of each insular seed (Lat.: *insula,* island) labor-intensive
to the max. Cock, clit, haircut, union card, Latin, Old Norse—

where does any of it get us, I ask you. It's all so damned runic.
Though have you noticed with Whitman Samplers, how
the caramels are in one corner and the nougats in another,
and you can see the curve of the cashews peeking through
the bittersweet, saying in shards of cashew-speak, *pick me.*

Free Hermit Crab

Or light, the relic of farewells.

—WALLACE STEVENS

Under the left half
of the moon, fish-smell
comes in on the sea,
in on long green ribbons
like a childhood hour.

You want to blend in
with the men dangling
lines off the pier,
but signs everywhere
squawk *difference:*

undulating anchors
on blue-collar biceps,
tough white guys
singing black blues
beneath the ratty palms,

QWIK MART, KWIK
MART, SAY YES!
TO JESUS, Pleasure
Island Plaza, Jubilee
Amusement Park

(each night a clown,
orange hair igniting the sky,
gives every child under ten
a free hermit crab).
Soon the sun will hover

like a Sunday wafer
before a pious mouth.
Maybe you'll try
the chipped beef, grit
your teeth, a sort

of *risor sardonicus*,
mimicking the grin
of the gulls overhead,
or better yet, find yourself
some clean spit of sand

where an empty shell
or pack of Luckies
might shelter
your two pincers,
your eight knobby legs.

Marvelous the Myriad Forms

1. A Wave of Shapes

Marvelous the myriad forms of the leaf—
elliptic, lanceolate, linear—they loaf
or luff, a wave of shapes above the loam—
pinnate, palmate, sagittate—above the foam—
lyrate, runcinate, deltoid—each form
haven to aphid, beetle, or some little worm.

2. That Mound of Flame

Lava flows, slows, turns hard,
like fingers of a bony hand.
That mound of flame atop our land
sent glowing tendrils out, thick not lank,
so white-hot to start, so like love: lack
of heat will always click shut the lock,
consign us to a bed of rock.

3. Floe to Floe

This too will go, the seer avers, *a blur.*
You mock her claim. It's calm and blue
on your crystalline, inland sea. No clue
that through your chimney's dormant flue
Arctic air will blow, and you'll be cast, floe
to floe, dreaming of oleander and aloe.

4. The Tapering Trail

What force makes us forsake our first home?
For some, it's a distant city's lures, for some,
like Moses, it's the tidal pull of the Sole
Voice. For those who remain, it's the fire sale
of a mother's breath, the tapering trail of salt
bled into the rapid river, the body's silt,
a breeze blowing curtains from the window sill.

The Odd Morphology of Regret

Lint collector, abdominal eye, perpetual
seat of kindergarten curiosity—
insie or *outsie?*—

you reign: universally mammalian, very
center of our being, mute remnant
of Mom long after Mom's

become remnant, invaginated marker
of life's arc. (Insie and outsie
inexorably recede.)

But please, tell us, Señor Umbilicus,
Miss B. Button, why you lack
those frissons of feeling

that got us here, you who should be
the ultimate pleasure zone—
shapely, accessible,

clitoral, to whom reams of paeans
would certainly be penned—
why you remain so

utterly unerogenous, ghost port
where all the great vessels
once docked.

Calamari

Listen my son, this is
how it's going to be—one day
you'll be racing from work
at dusk and pass a blue sign
for a restaurant called *Mykonos*
and you'll remember the *you*
of today, the woman
you're late for, Janice or Jane,
will understand if you pause,
facing the sea of white-
washed wall, the windmill, the shore-
front café where you first tasted
ouzo and squid, *calamari*
they said and you said
the next thirty years,
though you never returned
(though the generals fled),
and the woman you loved
for her self and her laugh
and her yet-bandaged wrists
left the breeze
that still blows over your body
at odd times like this.

Parting Conversation

What can you say to your long-
time friend and former lover
who asks do you think much
about death except yes?
She asks because a rare
growth is choking her sacrum.
She tells you she is standing
before a closet door. She means
they are staging her next play
next February and February
is six months away. Her face
shows the sallow full moon
of palliation. You sit other-
wise silent on the back deck.
What you want to say is no.

My Woman Is Like Nevada,

sitting on California's long bent
knee the way a small girl sits
on Santa's lap at White Flint Mall,
telling that old man she's been good.
We both know it's a lie, like the promise
hissing between a chorine's thighs,
but it's a white lie,
the only white thing flaking the ground
in the dead of December in the desert.
And it's the season of lies,
so Santa reaches deep into his burlap sack
and gives her a starter's pistol, a waterfall,
a kiss—just what she wanted,
hard and wet and true.

Autumn Geometric

Must be another whitewashed wafer's
slithered through the slot of the celestial
jukebox: a drachma or piastre or shekel,
coin of the realm in some sere yet ever-
inhabited ancient land. Enter the theme,
borne on strings—bouzouki or oud,
dark fingers schooled in the eternal
minor key of rain, dust and olive tree.
Heat rises, worlds turn, leaves shudder
in wind, apples fall in the fullness of fall.
And in all this Earth's thousand lacerated,
lacerating tongues—in field, souk,
or shopping mall—skin of the fruit
yields to the teeth and flesh concedes
the juices that slide down your throat.

See You

I keep my passport in this box
of cherrywood: ruby-stained,
and no larger than a large man's
hand. He gave it to me knowing

full how little time remained.
He must have been thinking
it would remind me to do
something useful with my life.

He'd be here now if he hadn't
volunteered to be a relief doc
in Kuwait—that chemical pall
charring the sky, blotting the sun

for weeks, wreaking havoc on DNA.
Beneath the high arched doorway
to his house, he leans heavily
on his cane, forty years of bones,

steady gaze. He beats the hollowing
box of his chest twice, meaning
to tell me he's got me inside—
but he doesn't, the airport taxi does.

—Dr. Roelf Padt, 1956–1996,
Médecins Sans Frontières/Holland

Home Run

Somewhere still it's Salami Day,
so my father must be slicing and dicing

with the precision of a Japanese chef,
the chunks of purple meat flecked

with fat piling higher and higher
on the Formica counter in the kitchen.

If it's Tuesday, it'll be French Fry Day:
my friends will be hooking their mitts

to their jeans, hopping onto their bikes.
6 P.M.: he's been sighted again,

disgorged from the Dexter-Davison bus.
His briefcase moves in pace with his stride,

up the street toward our first-floor flat.
They can see the tie already loosened

at his neck, the sleeves of his white-
on-white shirt rolled back, baring

the lipomas that line the length
of his dark forearms like eroded hills.

They can already hear his chortle,
can imagine the gurgle of hot oil

surging through the mesh strainer.
Already they're burning the roofs

of their mouths, they'll never learn—
and the golden, hand-hewn fries, edges

beveled like cut gems, always taste
like luck. Sweat pearls on his scalp:

a windshield's first drops of rain,
wiped away, returning. It's the sweat

of running the bases, the ball rolling
between left and center all the way

to the fence. It's the good sweat of
a good man: my father, headed home.

Morning Flight

In a distant city a boy once shared the pig
Wilbur's dismay at all Charlotte's children
streaming from the barnyard that first day

of spring. Like so many jellyfish riding
currents of the Coral Sea, the baby spiders
lifted away from him, into the sunlit breeze.

Today, at a meeting where talk is of profit
and loss, a man thinks of insects he's known—
tiny ants tugging grains of sugar homeward,

mornings in his kitchen, migrating Monarchs
gowning the grove near Santa Cruz in orange
and black silk, a host of spiders in an April

barnyard—and wonders, as he peers through
frosted panes of aqua glass, if enough webbing
remains within to wind, unwind, cast off again.

Squid's Sex Life Revealed in USA TODAY

"Deep Sea Mystery Solved"

They say, *mi amigo*, genus *Architeuthis*,
giant male squid, you "measure 45 feet long
and would make calamari rings bigger
than a tractor tire."
                    (Sautéed in olive oil,
spread over a steaming bed of rice,
you'd sate a hungry battalion—lie low,
mon ami, down there in your inky cavern,
half a mile below the sizzling woks.)

They say you "use an extremely muscular
penis, three feet long and functioning
like a rivet or nail gun," that your "encounters
are infrequent and chance."

When passing a female "like two ships
in the night"
                    (apologies, my friend,
for the unbounded human appetite
for seafood and cliché),
                    they say you "quickly
maneuver to hammer into one of her arms
and inject under hydraulic pressure,
your six-inch line of sperm
undulating in the pitch."

At last they've captured the bare details,
but what do the scientists know of squid-time,
of how fast your waiting for her passes
in the safe cold depths,
and how love's tentacles hold.

La Création

Naked, from out the blue vortex,
a grown man lightly borne
in a blue-winged angel's arms
bends his head to the staggering light,
a man newly born, looking
to the world above, the world
of fish and the yellow moon
and the woman curved like a giant red ear,
the red sun, swirling, blown
out of an angel's horn,
the ram-headed man with the red Torah,
the shtetl, the rabbi, the ladder,
the menorah's nine lemony flames,
the purple-breasted women,
the blue lyre held by the blue king,
the donkey, lion, goat,
the golden fish with hands for fins,
the bearded butterfly. Above,
above His Son swaying on the white Cross,
flaccid abdomen covered at the groin
by a gray-fringed prayer shawl,
above it all, disembodied, two hands,
the visible hands of hiding
God, proffer twin tablets shaped
like pale loaves, or gravestones,
and I put my arm around my new wife's waist,
and she puts her arm around mine,
and we hold like that a minute
in that white room, in that white light,
infinite wavelets of white light.

Notes

Sto Lat. The ninth stanza's italicized segment is taken from Robert Desnos's eponymous poem, "The Voice of Robert Desnos," *The Selected Poems of Robert Desnos*, translated by Carolyn Forché and William Kulik (New York: Ecco Press, 1991). The Gestapo arrested Desnos in 1944 because of his activities in support of the French Resistance. He died of typhus at Terezin in 1945, as World War II was ending.

Passover. Upon the dissolution of the Ottoman Empire in the early part of the twentieth century, Smyrna, cosmopolitan and polyglot, became Izmir, Turkey. *"Ochi Tchornya,"* or "Dark Eyes," is a well-known Russian folk song about the yearning for, and impossibility of, love across cultures.

This Way to the Egress. This poem takes its title from the practice of the nineteenth-century American huckster/showman, P. T. Barnum. Among the many "exotic feature exhibits" he offered was the Egress. Signs advertising its availability for paid viewing were similar to those for other marvels such as Tom Thumb, the India Rubber Man and the Half-Man-Half-Woman. To see the Egress, people would buy tickets, follow the signs and arrive at the rear alley, their exit from the Carnival hastened.

There Is No Point in Time. The French sentence, phrase, and word mean, respectively, *To part is to die a little, cat's cry,* and *nothing.*

Free Hermit Crab. *Risor sardonicus,* Latin for "sardonic smile," is sign of the trismus pathognomonic to tetanus, to which the disease owes its popular name, "lockjaw."